SALVE
REGINA

BISHOP ATHANASIUS SCHNEIDER

SALVE REGINA

A ROSARY CRUSADE TO PLEAD FOR HOLY POPES

SOPHIA INSTITUTE PRESS

Manchester, New Hampshire

CONTENTS

INTRODUCTION 7
PRAYER TO PLEAD FOR HOLY POPES 13
LITANY OF THE CHILD JESUS 15

JOYFUL MYSTERIES
The First Joyful Mystery 23
The Second Joyful Mystery 27
The Third Joyful Mystery 33
The Fourth Joyful Mystery 39
The Fifth Joyful Mystery 45

SORROWFUL MYSTERIES
The First Sorrowful Mystery 53
The Second Sorrowful Mystery 59
The Third Sorrowful Mystery 65
The Fourth Sorrowful Mystery 71
The Fifth Sorrowful Mystery 77

GLORIOUS MYSTERIES
The First Glorious Mystery 85
The Second Glorious Mystery 91
The Third Glorious Mystery 97
The Fourth Glorious Mystery 103
The Fifth Glorious Mystery 109

About the Author 115

INTRODUCTION

Over the centuries, many holy popes have constantly recommended the prayer of the Rosary. In the apparitions at Fátima in Portugal, Our Lady stressed the importance of this devotion. In her final apparition, on October 13, 1917, she declared: "I am the Queen of the Rosary."

Regarding the significance of the Rosary and its spiritual efficacy, the Servant of God Sr. Lúcia of Fátima expressed herself as follows:

The Most Holy Virgin, in these times in which we live, has given a new efficacy to the prayer of the Holy Rosary. She has granted us that efficacy in such a way that there is no problem, no matter how difficult it may be — whether temporal or, above all, spiritual — in the personal lives of each one of us or of our families … that cannot be resolved by the Rosary. … There is no problem, I tell you, no matter how difficult it may be, that we cannot resolve through the prayer of the Holy Rosary. (Interview of Sister Lúcia of Fátima with Fr. Fuentes, December 26, 1957)

Our holy Mother Church suffers in the present from an unprecedented crisis that affects her entire body: faith, moral life, pastoral and clerical life, the sacred liturgy, and even the highest echelons of the Church hierarchy. The Holy See, whose essential mission is to be the Chair of Truth, is partially occupied by her enemies, who have succeeded in exerting a decisive influence on the Roman Curia itself — on the very governance of the Catholic Church.

Just as in 1570, at the Battle of Lepanto — when, against all human hope, Europe was freed from the enemies of the Catholic Faith through the prayer of the Rosary — today, too, we are called to unite in a new Rosary crusade, begging God to free the Holy See from subjection to Christ's enemies. May He grant us an era guided by holy popes who do not fear worldly powers, who make no compromises with the spirit of the age, but rather who preserve, strengthen, and defend the Catholic Faith, even to the point of shedding their own blood. May they also safeguard, protect, and pass on the venerable liturgy of the Roman Church.

When all human help seems to be vanity, God is pleased to come to our aid through the little ones, for "God chose what is weak in the world to shame the strong. . . . so that no human being might boast in the presence of God" (1 Cor. 1:27, 29). Therefore, even though one may be an adult, whoever takes part in this crusade should consider himself, before God and within himself, to be a little one. In the life of the Church, these little ones are like the *Galanthus nivalis* flower — known as the snowdrop — which is called the "little bell of spring," for its blossoming heralds the coming of spring.

May an army of little ones, through this crusade, offer to the Queen of the Most Holy

Rosary a crown of these "spring bells." She, who is like an "army set in array" (*acies ordinata*), will deliver the Roman Curia from the enemies of the Catholic Faith by means of a new host of many holy popes. We believe in the Catholic Church, against which the gates of Hell shall never prevail.

May 13, 2024, Feast of Our Lady of Fátima
✠ Bishop Athanasius Schneider,
Auxiliary Bishop of the Archdiocese
of Mary Most Holy in Astana

PRAYER TO PLEAD
FOR HOLY POPES

Kyrie Eleison! Christe Eleison! Kyrie Eleison! Lord Jesus Christ, You are the Good Shepherd! With Your most powerful hand, You lead Your pilgrim Church through the storms of this valley of tears.

Adorn the Holy See with holy popes who neither fear the authority of this world nor compromise with the spirit of the age, but who preserve, strengthen, and defend the Catholic Faith, even to the point of shedding their own blood; and who honor, protect, and pass on the venerable liturgy of the Roman Church.

O Lord, watch over us through holy popes, aflame with the zeal of the apostles, who proclaim to the whole world: "There is salvation in no one else, for there is no other name under heaven given among men by which we must be saved" (Acts 4:12).

Through an era of holy popes, may the Holy See — which is the homeland of all who profess the Catholic and apostolic Faith — ever shine forth as the Chair of Truth for the whole world. Hear us, Lord, and by the intercession of the Immaculate Heart of Mary, who is Mother of the Church, grant us holy popes, grant us many holy popes! Have mercy on us and hear us! Amen.

LITANY OF THE CHILD JESUS

Lord, have mercy on us.

Jesus Christ, have mercy on us.

Lord, have mercy on us.

Jesus Christ, hear us.

Jesus Christ, graciously hear us.

God the Father of Heaven, *have mercy on us.*

God the Son, Redeemer of the world,

God the Holy Spirit,

Holy Trinity, one God,

Child Jesus Christ, *have mercy on us.*

Child, true God,

Child, Son of the living God,

Child, Son of the Virgin Mary,

Child, mighty in weakness,

Child, powerful in tenderness,

Child, treasury of grace,

Child, fountain of love,

Child, renewer of Heaven,

Child, restorer of the world's ills,

Child, head of the angels,

Child, root of the patriarchs,

Child, fulfillment of the prophets,

Child, desire of the Gentiles,

Child, joy of the shepherds,

Child, light of the Magi,

Child, salvation of children,

Child, the hope of the righteous,

Child, teacher of the wise,

Child, firstfruits of all the saints,

Be merciful to us, forgive us, O Child Jesus.
Be merciful to us, hear us, O Child Jesus.

From the slavery of the children of Adam,
deliver us, O Child Jesus.
From bondage to the devil,
From the evil desires of the flesh,
From the malice of the world,
From the pride of life,
From the inordinate desire for knowledge,
From blindness of spirit,
From ill will,
From our sins,
By Your most pure Conception,
By Your humble Birth,
By Your tears,
By Your painful Circumcision,
By Your glorious Epiphany,
By Your holy Presentation in the Temple,

By Your most divine life,

By Your poverty,

By Your many sufferings,

By Your labors and journeys,

Lamb of God, Who take away the sins of the world, spare us, O Child Jesus.

Lamb of God, Who take away the sins of the world, graciously hear us, O Child Jesus.

Lamb of God, Who take away the sins of the world, have mercy on us.

O Child Jesus, hear us.

O Child Jesus, graciously hear us.

Let us pray.

Lord Jesus Christ, You willed so greatly to humble Yourself in Your incarnate divinity and sacred humanity that You were born in time and became a little child. Grant that we may recognize infinite wisdom in the silence of a child, power in weakness, and majesty in humility. May we, by adoring Your self-abasement on earth, come to contemplate Your glory in Heaven, You Who, with the Father and the Holy Spirit, live and reign forever and ever. Amen.

Joyful
Mysteries

THE ANNUNCIATION

The Annunciation of the Angel Gabriel to the Virgin Mary

In this mystery, we contemplate how Almighty God, after the announcement of the angel Gabriel to the Virgin Mary, came down from Heaven and became truly man — body and soul — in the womb of the Immaculate Virgin Mary. This took place in the little town of Nazareth in Galilee, in the purest Mother of God's humble room. Having received the name of Jesus, meaning "Savior," He — Who is the ineffable, eternal, and infinite Word and Son of God — was made flesh and began to dwell among us.

Before becoming man, God asked for humanity's consent, since He does not impose His salvation or His love on us. No one can be forced to love. God deigned to request that consent in the mystery of the Annunciation, and the Virgin Mary consented on behalf of all mankind. With her pure heart, she uttered her yes, filled with faith and trust. Mary's yes is the perfect antithesis to the no of Eve, the first woman, who disobeyed God and sinned, becoming the cause of the perdition of all humanity. Mary's yes, on the contrary, made her the cause of humanity's salvation.

At the moment of the Incarnation, the Holy Spirit formed the most pure body and soul of Jesus. Therefore, the Virgin Mary had to be perfectly immaculate, since from her flesh the body of Christ — the incarnate

God — would be formed. Already in the first instant of His life in the Immaculate Virgin's womb, Jesus enjoyed the Beatific Vision and knew all things. Thus, from the very first moment of His earthly life, Jesus beheld and embraced, with immense love, all human beings — each one of us. From then on, Jesus and Mary, in the work of humanity's Redemption, never parted; they remain together for all eternity. In light of such a sublime truth, may we, here on earth, remain united to them, so that this union may continue in Heaven forever.

Lord, by the mystery of the Annunciation of Your Incarnation, grant us holy popes! Grant us many holy popes! Amen.

THE VISITATION

The Virgin Mary Visits Her Cousin Elizabeth

The angel Gabriel greeted the Virgin Mary and told her that her elderly cousin Elizabeth was already in her sixth month of pregnancy. That alone sufficed for the Mother of the Savior to leave everything and travel quickly to her relative's home to assist her, not minding that she would have to walk almost one hundred miles. In this episode, we see how great Mary's love for her neighbor truly was. It was the fire of Jesus' love, borne by her first in her soul rather than in her womb, that moved her to perform this great work of charity. As St. Augustine put it: "Mary, full of grace, conceived Jesus first in her heart before conceiving Him in her womb" (see *Sermo* 215, 4).

From the moment of the Incarnation, no one was ever as intimately united to Christ as Mary was. Hers was a life of intense union with God — a genuine spiritual life — and never for a single moment was she indifferent to her neighbor. St. Francis de Sales said: "We know that one same charity extends itself to both the love of God and our neighbour, raising us to the union of our spirit with God, and bringing us back again to a loving society with our neighbours" (*Treatise on the Love of God*, X, 11).

The Virgin Mary shows us an example of humility and profound delicacy. Despite being the true Mother of God, she forgot herself and took the initiative to greet Elizabeth.

In this mystery of the Visitation, we see a great truth: Mary is the Mediatrix of the graces of the Redeemer. Her voice became the instrument of John the Baptist's sanctification in his mother's womb, as well as of Elizabeth's enlightenment by the Holy Spirit. In that most holy encounter, for the first time we hear from a human mouth the divinely revealed truth that Mary is the Mother of God, when Elizabeth calls her "the Mother of my Lord" — for the Jewish people, the word *Lord* (in Hebrew *Adonai* and *Yahweh*) meant "God."

Finally, in visiting Elizabeth, the Virgin Mary left us one of the most beautiful hymns of praise, the Magnificat, in which these golden words shine forth: "All generations shall call me blessed." Not only all generations of human beings but also all the angels will call her blessed for all eternity. May we always act with charity, humility, and zeal to honor Mary.

Lord, by the mystery of the Visitation, grant us holy popes! Grant us many holy popes! Amen.

THE NATIVITY

The Birth of Jesus in Bethlehem

In the grotto of Bethlehem, where Jesus was born, something occurred that no human being could ever have imagined: the almighty, boundless, and eternal God—Who "dwells in unapproachable light, whom no man has ever seen or can see" (1 Tim. 6:16)—became visible. By becoming man, God did not appear as a strong, already grown, adult figure; rather, He appeared as all of us once were: as a fragile newborn baby. Why did God choose to appear among us in this way? To manifest

His immense love for us, so as to draw us to Himself and kindle in us the fire of His love, the love of heavenly things, just as Holy Church prays: "That, in coming to know God visibly, we may be caught up in love of what is invisible" (Preface of Christmas). "When the goodness and loving kindness of God our Savior appeared, he saved us" (Titus 3:4).

God wanted to show His love in an even more compelling way. He was born in utter poverty, among animals, outside the city, for He found no one to take Him in. "He came to his own home, and his own people recei-ved him not." (John 1:11). The birth of Jesus revealed not only God's ineffable love but also His humility. As St. Augustine writes: "The One who holds the world in being was lying in a manger; he was simultaneously speechless infant and Word. … O manifest infirmity and wondrous humility in which was thus concealed total divinity! … May he bring his gifts to perfection in us, since he did not shrink from making his own our tiny beginnings" (*Sermo* 184, 3).

And St. Bernard exclaimed, "The more He humbles Himself on my account, the more powerfully He engages my love" (*Sermo* 1 in *Epiphania Domini*, 2).

The Divine Child — God, Who is love and humility — lying in the manger, was first adored with profound faith and love by Mary Most Holy and St. Joseph, the purest and humblest creatures ever to dwell on earth, as well as by the most modest and forgotten of society, the simple shepherds. Let us implore Jesus to be born always in our hearts through our acts of faith and love. Angelus Silesius once said: "If Christ were born in Bethlehem a thousand times and not in thee thyself; then art thou lost eternally" (*Der Cherubinische Wandersmann*, I, 61).

St. Francis of Assisi would often exclaim, "Let us love the Child of Bethlehem!"

Lord, by the mystery of Your Birth in Bethlehem, grant us holy popes! Grant us many holy popes! Amen.

THE PRESENTATION

The Presentation of the Child Jesus in the Temple of Jerusalem

The Child Jesus was taken by Mary Most Holy and St. Joseph to the Temple to be presented to God, showing us that we were created to belong to Him at all times and for all eternity. Jesus was brought to the Temple made of stone in Jerusalem, even though His own body is the true temple of the Divinity, for in Him "all the fulness of God was pleased to dwell" (Col. 1:19).

Mary and Joseph offered as a sacrifice two turtledoves. In Sacred Scripture, the dove symbolizes the Holy Spirit, Who brought forth and anointed the sacred humanity of Jesus, guided Him in all His redemptive work, and dwells within His humanity — the instrument of our salvation.

In the Temple at Jerusalem, the incarnate God encountered His people in two of their most worthy representatives: the elderly Simeon and the prophetess Anna, who likewise represented both sexes, since all people are called to consecrate themselves to God. St. Ambrose wrote: "Every age and both sexes, along with the miracles that occur, confirm our faith: the Virgin (Mary) gives birth, the barren (Elizabeth) conceives, the mute (Zechariah) speaks, Elizabeth prophesies, the Magus adores, John leaps in the womb, the widow (Anna) confesses, the righteous man (Simeon) waits" (*In Luc. II*, 2).

In the Temple, Simeon declared Christ to be the divine light illuminating all peoples and nations, but also a sign of contradiction. For that reason, the Church and every true Christian must likewise be a sign of contradiction to sin and the world, with which we cannot be friends. During the Presentation of the Child Jesus, we see the first reference to the Immaculate Heart of Mary, which would be pierced by the sword of compassion for her Redeemer Son and by the countless sins of humanity.

Christ, presented in the Temple, comes forth to meet us. Let us run to meet Him with the good works of faith and charity. Like Simeon, let us take Him in our arms with heartfelt and profound love.

Lord, by the mystery of Your Presentation in the Temple, grant us holy popes! Grant us many holy popes! Amen.

THE FINDING OF JESUS
IN THE TEMPLE

The Child Jesus Is Found in the Temple of Jerusalem

After three days of anguished searching, Mary and St. Joseph finally find the Child Jesus in the Temple of Jerusalem. In that moment, the Virgin began to share in her sorrowful soul the redemptive mission of her Divine Son. Even though He was still a boy, Christ reveals to His Mother the mission He must fulfill when He says: "I must be in my Father's house?" (Luke 2:49). The Father's house is what Jesus would mean later when he said: "My food is to do the will of him who sent me, and to accomplish his work" (John 4:34). This work means that Jesus offers Himself in sacrifice to redeem all mankind. When speaking with the doctors of the Law in the Temple, the Divine Child likewise reveals His mission to be the one true Teacher of humanity, as He will later proclaim: "You have one teacher.... You have one master, the Christ" (Matt. 23:8, 10).

Though He was the eternal God, Jesus offered an example of submission and obedience in entrusting Himself to the care of Mary Most Holy and St. Joseph: "He went down with them and came to Nazareth and was obedient to them" (Luke 2:51). God Himself — Who gave us the command to honor father and mother — provided the noblest example of its faithful fulfillment.

St. Bernard said: "Who was subject? God, to man. God to Whom the angels are subject. God, Whom the powers and principalities obey, was subject to Mary. And not only to Mary, but to Joseph also for Mary's sake. Consider, then, and choose which you will most admire, the gracious condescension of the Son, or the surpassing dignity of the mother. Both are amazing; both are miraculous. That a God should obey a woman is humility without example; that a woman should command the Son of God is a dignity without parallel. In the praise of virgins we hear that wonderful verse: 'They shall follow the Lamb whithersoever he goeth.' But what praise, think you, is worthy of her who leads the way before Him? Learn, O man, to obey; learn, O earth, to be subject; learn, O dust, to be submissive" (*Sermo* 1, *Super missus est*).

In this mystery, God also reveals to us the beauty and the importance of the Christian family, which finds its highest model in the Holy Family of Jesus, Mary, and Joseph.

"If the man is the head, the woman is the heart, and as he occupies the chief place in ruling, so she may and ought to claim for herself the chief place in love.… The family is more sacred than the State.… Men are begotten not for the earth and for time, but for Heaven and eternity" (Pope Pius XI, Encyclical *Casti Connubii*).

Lord, by the power of the mystery of the Holy Family, grant us holy popes! Grant us many holy popes! Amen.

Sorrowful Mysteries

THE AGONY IN
THE GARDEN

The Agony of Jesus in the Garden of Olives

Jesus Christ, our incarnate God, experienced in His human soul the full reality of agony, of fear in the face of death: "His sweat became like great drops of blood falling down upon the ground" (Luke 22:44). He suffered to the point that He asked the Father to take away the cup of suffering from Him. Immediately, however, He added those golden words: "Nevertheless not my will, but thine, be done" (Luke 22:42). In this way, Jesus showed that He indeed possessed a fully human will and acted as a man, without opposing the divine will: "The Word made flesh willed humanly in obedience to the Father all that He had decided divinely with the Father and the Holy Spirit for our salvation. Christ's human will 'does not resist or oppose but rather submits to His divine and almighty will.'" (*Catechism of the Catholic Church*, 475)

"Jesus will be in agony even to the end of the world. We must not sleep during that time" (Blaise Pascal, *Pensées*, no. 552). In Gethsemane, Jesus suffered especially on account of the sins of His ministers: of the popes, bishops, priests, and religious. He revealed this to St. Padre Pio: "During my agony, my son, nobody should sleep. My soul goes in search of a drop of human compassion but alas, I am left alone beneath the weight of indifference. The ingratitude and the sleep of my ministers makes my agony all the more grievous. Alas, how little they correspond to my love! What afflicts me most is that they add contempt and unbelief to their indifference" (Letter to Fr. Agostino, April 7, 1913).

Yet Christ's deepest sorrow in the Garden of Olives was seeing the souls that would be lost forever.

The incarnate God deigned to let Himself be helped and consoled by His creatures: "There appeared to him an angel from heaven, strengthening him" (Luke 22:43). This angelic aid included all acts of reparation that would be offered over time — through prayers and spiritual or physical sufferings of expiation — by countless devout souls.

Jesus said to St. Margaret Mary Alacoque: "Here in this place (Gethsemane), I suffered more interiorly than in the rest of my Passion, because I was totally alone, abandoned by heaven and earth, burdened with the sins of humanity.... Arise between eleven and midnight and prostrate yourself in adoration with me for an hour" (*Vie et Révélations de Sainte Marguerite-Marie Alacoque, écrites par elle-même*, chap. III).

Let us strive to console Jesus, especially during holy hours of adoration.

Lord, by the mystery of Your Agony in the Garden of Olives, grant us holy popes! Grant us many holy popes! Amen.

THE SCOURGING

The Scourging of Jesus

Jesus is cruelly scourged. We can get an idea of what this scourging was really like from the witness of the Shroud of Turin. Scientific analysis has concluded that Jesus was tied to a column; afterward, they whipped His back, chest, and legs with a scourge consisting of two or three leather straps with metal balls at the tips. Again and again, these metal tips dug deeply into His most holy flesh, tearing His skin, blood vessels, nerves, and muscles. His mouth was dry, and His tongue clung to the roof of His mouth. Since the Romans carried out the scourging, they did not observe the Jewish law limiting lashes to forty minus one. Jesus was brutally whipped by two executioners, who inflicted more than 120 blows on Him.

"How must the angels be astonished to see the Incarnate Word doing such horrible penance in His immaculate flesh for the foul sins committed by us in our flesh? How much more astonished ought we to be to know that a God is so scourged and mangled in His human nature for our carnal sins? Although not God, but only the flesh united with God, suffers, the pain of the flesh still redounds on God Himself. How great an evil, then, must be the sin of impurity, since it is punished with so great severity in the most pure flesh of a God? How deadly must be the wounds of sense, since there is no balsam to heal them but the blood issuing from the wounds of a Man-God?" (Fr. Gaetano da Bergamo, *Thoughts and Affections on the Passion of Jesus Christ for Every Day of the Year*, chap. 49)

May we say to Our Lord Who was scourged: "Jesus, Lover of chastity, ardent Lover of chaste souls! I repent for having thus mangled Thee by my impurities. I implore of Thee the grace of pardon for the past and help for the future, that I may never more offend Thee. Remove from me the occasions of sin, strengthen me to conquer temptations and my disorderly passions. Extinguish in me the desires of the flesh, and grant me that holy spirit by which I may be restrained from ever again offending against chastity, but, on the contrary, may love and guard it with all possible jealousy" (Ibid.)

When Teresa of Ávila once contemplated Jesus scourged, she was converted once and for all:

It came to pass one day, when I went into the oratory, that I saw a picture which they had put by there. … It was a representation of Christ most grievously wounded; and so devotional, that the very sight of it, when I saw it, moved me — so well did it show forth that which He suffered for us. So keenly did I feel the evil return I had made for those wounds, that I thought my heart was breaking. I threw myself on the ground beside it, my tears flowing plenteously, and implored Him to strengthen me once for all, so that I might never offend Him any more. (*The Life of St. Teresa of Jesus*, 9, 1)

Lord, by the power of the mystery of Your scourging, grant us holy popes! Grant us many holy popes! Amen.

THE CROWING
WITH THORNS

The Crowning with Thorns

In this moment of His holy Passion, Jesus is reduced to the most humiliating state, for He is crowned with thorns, dressed in ragged purple garments, mockingly acclaimed as a king, and treated like a fool. The thorns pierce His head from all sides, nearly crushing His eyes. All the veins of His head are punctured; blood flows like water from this newly opened spring. Let us consider the countless pains — and the intensity of those pains — brought on by dozens of extremely sharp thorns that tore into the nerve endings, not only of the skin but also of all the layers of soft tissue in the scalp, reaching even into His skull itself. Then we will be able, in some small way, to grasp the pain caused by the crowning with thorns. It is said that there were about seventy thorns, each an inch and a half long.

In the sufferings of His crowning with thorns, Our Lord atones not only for sins of pride but also for blasphemies. "The crowning with thorns was the atonement for the sins of the mind — for the atheists who wish there were no God, for the doubters whose evil lives becloud their thinking, for the egotists, centered on themselves. The soldiers cursed as the thorns pricked their fingers. Then they cursed the Lord, as they drove the crown of thorns into His head, as a mockery of a royal diadem....

In this Mystery is verified the truth of our Saviour's warning: 'If the world hates you, be sure that it hated Me before it learned to hate you. If you belonged to the world, the world would know you for its own and love you; it is because you do not belong to the world, because I have singled you out from the midst of the world, that the world hates you.' He who expects to preserve his faith without being mocked by the world is either weak in it, or else not so bold in goodness as to draw upon himself the mocking insults of another purple robe and a torturing circle of thorns" (Archbishop Fulton Sheen, *Meditations on the 15 Mysteries of the Rosary*).

According to St. Augustine: "So great is the beneficence of human humility, that even the Divine Majesty was pleased to commend it by His own example" (*In Ioan.* tr.

55, 7). Thus, in the mystery of the Crowning with Thorns, we want to learn — and pray for the grace of — a truly profound humility.

Lord, by the mystery of Your crowning with thorns, grant us holy popes! Grant us many holy popes! Amen.

JESUS CARRIES THE CROSS

Jesus Carries the Cross

In this mystery, we see the practical fulfillment of Isaiah's prophecy: "Surely he has borne our griefs and carried our sorrows; yet we esteemed him stricken, smitten by God, and afflicted" (Isa. 53:4). The heavy cross He carried on His shoulders caused Him a new and extremely painful wound: the wound of the shoulder.

One unmistakable mark of a disciple of Christ is the acceptance of the cross, imitating His example, for He said: "Take up your cross!" It is not a request or a piece of advice but a command so unyielding that our salvation depends on its faithful observance. "He who does not take his cross and follow me is not worthy of me" (Matt. 10:38). "Jesus hath many lovers of His heavenly kingdom, but few bearers of His Cross" (Thomas à Kempis, *The Imitation of Christ*, II, 11).

St. Charles Borromeo used to say: "I salute thee, O precious cross, I salute thee, O blessed tribulation! O holy affliction, how delightful thou art, since thou didst issue from the loving breast of this Father of eternal mercy, who willed thee from all eternity, and ordained thee for my dear people and me! O cross, my heart wills thee, since the heart of my God has willed thee; O cross, my soul cherishes and embraces thee, with its whole affection!" (St. Francis de Sales, *Treatise on the Love of God*, XII, 9).

Jesus promised that we will never be abandoned in difficulties if we trust in Him: "I can do all things in him who strengthens me" (Phil. 4:13). Every true Christian—and the entire Church—is distinguished by imitating Christ on His path of the Holy Cross. God has decreed that we reach the light of salvation and true happiness only by accepting Christ's cross in our lives. For the life of every true Christian and of the whole Church, these words of St. Augustine ring true: The Church advances on her pilgrimage amid the persecutions of the world and the consolations of God (see *De civ. Dei*, 18, 51).

In the words of St. John Mary Vianney: "There are two ways of suffering—to suffer with love, and to suffer without love. The saints suffered everything with joy, patience, and perseverance, because they loved. As for us, we suffer with anger, vexation, and weariness, because we do not love. If we loved God, we should love crosses, we should wish for them, we should take pleasure in them. … We should be happy to be able to suffer for the love of Him who lovingly suffered for us" (*Instructions on the Catechism*, chap. 18: Catechesis on Suffering).

Lord, by the mystery of Your Way of the Cross, grant us holy popes! Grant us many holy popes! Amen.

THE CRUCIFIXION

The Crucifixion and Death of Jesus

"He could have redeemed us in a thousand other ways than that of His Son's death. But He did not will to do so, for what may have been sufficient for our salvation was not sufficient for His love; and to show us how much He loved us, this divine Son died the cruelest and most ignominious of deaths, that of the Cross." (St. Francis de Sales, *Sermon for Good Friday*, March 25, 1622).

We were redeemed by the blood of His Cross (see Col. 1:20). "But one of the soldiers pierced his side with a spear, and at once there came out blood and water" (John 19:34). This water and blood symbolizes Baptism and the Eucharist, respectively. It is from these sacraments that Holy Church was born — by the cleansing waters of rebirth (Baptism) and by renewal in the Holy Spirit (the Eucharist), which flowed from the side of Christ. "It was from his side that Christ fashioned the Church, as he had fashioned Eve from the side of Adam" (St. John Chrysostom, *Cat.* 3, 18).

"In the Cross is heavenly sweetness, in the Cross strength of mind, in the Cross joy of the spirit, in the Cross the height of virtue, in the Cross perfection of holiness" (*The Imitation of Christ*, II, 12).

We must "complete what is lacking in Christ's afflictions" (Col. 1:24). We must suffer with Christ, conforming ourselves to Him by embracing the will of God with the depth of our being, as Abraham did when he was about to offer Isaac.

"If there had been no cross, life would not have been nailed to the wood with nails. If life had not been nailed, there would not have gushed forth from His side the streams of immortality — blood and water — that cleanse the world. The record of sin would not have been torn up; we would not have obtained the declaration of our freedom; we would not have tasted of the tree of life, nor would Paradise have been opened. If there had been no cross, death would not have been vanquished, nor hell defeated"

(St. Andrew of Crete, *Oratio 10 in Exaltatione sanctae crucis*).

May we unite ourselves every day to the sacrifice of the Holy Cross by offering this prayer in the morning: "O God, in union with the intentions of the Heart of Jesus on the Cross and in all the sacrifices of the Mass, I offer You this day — my thoughts, words, and deeds, my joys, setbacks, and sufferings — and I offer, with all the love I can muster, the moment of my death and all its circumstances, in reparation for my sins and for Your greater glory."

Lord, by the mystery of Your Holy Cross, grant us holy popes! Grant us many holy popes! Amen.

Glorious Mysteries

THE RESURRECTION

The Resurrection of Jesus

In the early hours of the third day after His death—that is, on the first day of the week—Jesus rose from the dead. From that time onward, this day has been called the Lord's Day, Sunday. By a unique act of His divine omnipotence—in union with the Father and the Holy Spirit—Jesus Christ reunited His soul with His body and arose from the tomb alive. Our Lord's Resurrection is supremely important, for it is the very foundation of our Faith (see 1 Cor. 15:14–17), the means by which the fruits of Redemption are applied to us (see 1 Pet.

1:3), the model of our spiritual life (see Rom. 6:4–11), and the cause of our future resurrection (see Rom. 6:5).

We read in a homily by St. Melito, Bishop of Sardis in the second century, how the risen Lord speaks to us: "I am your forgiveness, your saving Passover, the Lamb sacrificed for you, the water that purifies you, your life, your resurrection, your light, your salvation, your King. I will lead you to the heights, I will raise you up, and I will show you the Father who is in heaven; I will lift you up with My right hand" (*Homily on the Passover*).

Christ's Resurrection begins transforming our life on the day of Baptism. Being baptized, we are immersed in the water, as though buried to sin and death; emerging from the water, clothed in grace, we resemble Christ coming forth from the tomb in the glory of the Resurrection (see Col. 2:12). This life of grace entails a more intimate participation in Christ's life: "We were buried therefore with him by baptism into death, so that as Christ was raised from the dead by the glory of the Father, we too might walk in newness of life" (Rom. 6:4). By sharing in His sufferings, we become "like him in his death, that if possible I may attain the resurrection from the dead" (Phil. 3:10–11). Through that same participation, we grasp the sublime value of the precious blood that flowed from His wounds, which He wanted to retain in His risen body and bring with Him to Heaven to show God the Father the price of our Redemption (see St. Ambrose, *In Luc.* 10, 24).

We believe in the resurrection of the dead — of our mortal bodies. By living this new life in sanctifying grace, we experience a first spiritual resurrection and thus await the resurrection of our bodies at the end of the world (see St. Augustine, *In Ioann.* Tr. 19, 10).

Lord, by the mystery of Your Holy Resurrection, grant us holy popes! Grant us many holy popes! Amen.

THE ASCENSION

The Ascension of Jesus

Jesus said, "I am ascending to my Father and your Father, to my God and your God" (John 20:17). Forty days after His Resurrection, Jesus ascended into Heaven, taking with Him all the just of the Old Law, the souls in the limbo of the patriarchs. At the same time, Jesus is present in Heaven and on earth, but in different ways: in Heaven, bodily; on earth, truly present yet hidden under sacramental veils in the Most Blessed Sacrament of the Altar.

St. Augustine remarked: "Today our Lord Jesus Christ ascended into heaven; let our hearts ascend with him.... He did not leave heaven when he came down to us; nor did he withdraw from us when he went up again into heaven. The fact that he was in heaven even while he was on earth is borne out by his own statement: *No one has ever ascended into heaven except the one who descended from heaven, the Son of Man, who is in heaven"* (*Sermon on the Ascension of the Lord*).

Pope St. Leo the Great taught: "That which till then was visible of our Redeemer was changed into a sacramental presence, and that faith might be more excellent and stronger, sight gave way to doctrine, the authority of which was to be accepted by believing hearts enlightened with rays from above. This Faith, increased by the Lord's Ascension and established by the gift of the Holy Ghost, was not terrified by bonds, imprisonments, banishments, hunger, fire, attacks by wild beasts, refined torments of cruel persecutors. For this Faith throughout the world not only men, but even women, not only beardless boys, but even tender maids, fought to the shedding of their blood. This Faith cast out spirits, drove off sicknesses, raised the dead: and through it the blessed Apostles themselves also, who after being confirmed by so many miracles and instructed by so many discourses, had yet been panic-stricken by the horrors of the Lord's Passion and had not accepted the truth of His resurrection without hesitation, made such progress after the Lord's Ascension that everything which had previously filled them with fear was turned into joy" (*Sermon 2 on the Ascension*).

With God's grace, we want to believe and live according to the Apostle's teaching: "If then you have been raised with Christ, seek the things that are above, where Christ is, seated at the right hand of God. Set your minds on things that are above, not on things that are on earth" (Col. 3:1–2).

Lord, by the mystery of Your Holy Ascension, grant us holy popes! Grant us many holy popes! Amen.

PENTECOST

The Descent of the Holy Spirit on Pentecost

On Pentecost day, the Holy Spirit — the third Person of the Most Holy Trinity — visibly came down from Heaven in the form of tongues of fire that rested upon Our Lady, the apostles, and the other disciples gathered in the Upper Room in Jerusalem (see Acts 2:1–4). The Holy Spirit taught the apostles the fullness of truth and filled those who were weak and timid with the zeal of martyrs. Pentecost is the day on which the Church was first made manifest to the world; it is the beginning of her missionary expansion.

"'The Church which, already conceived, came forth from the side of the second Adam in His sleep on the Cross, first showed Herself before the eyes of men on the great day of Pentecost.' For the Divine Redeemer began the building of the mystical temple of the Church when by His preaching He made known His Precepts; He completed it when he hung glorified on the Cross; and He manifested and proclaimed it when He sent the Holy Ghost as Paraclete in visible form on His disciples" (Pope Pius XII, *Encyclical Mystici Corporis Christi*, 26).

Since the Holy Spirit is the love of the Father and of the Son, it is to Him in particular that we attribute the sanctification of souls. Pope St. Gregory the Great said:

"Today the Holy Spirit descended upon the disciples and changed their worldly minds, filling them with love for Him; and while tongues of fire appeared externally, they were inwardly set ablaze in their hearts. For while they received God in the form of fire, they were enveloped by the flames of His love. At the Nativity, God became man, assuming human nature; at Pentecost, men became gods by adoption" (*Homilies on the Gospel*, 30).

Christ is the Head of the Church, and the Holy Spirit is her soul: "What the soul is in our body, that is the Holy Ghost in Christ's body, the Church" (St. Augustine, *Serm.* 187, *de temp.*).

"We too receive the Holy Ghost if we love the Church," said St. Augustine (*In Ioan*, tr.

32, 8). St. Thomas Aquinas taught: "The soul acts virtuously and perfectly when she acts through charity, and through charity God lives in her; indeed, without charity she cannot act; for scripture says, *Whoever does not love, remains in death.* If a person possesses all the gifts of the Holy Spirit, but lacks charity, that person has no life" (*Opuscula theologica, In duo praecepta*).

Lord, by the mystery of the sending of the Holy Spirit on Pentecost, grant us holy popes! Grant us many holy popes! Amen.

THE ASSUMPTION OF MARY

The Assumption of Our Lady into Heaven

"Since our Redeemer is the Son of Mary, he could not do otherwise, as the perfect observer of God's law, than to honor, not only his eternal Father, but also his most beloved Mother.... Just as the glorious resurrection of Christ was an essential part and the final sign of this victory, so that struggle which was common to the Blessed Virgin and her divine Son should be brought to a close by the glorification of her virginal body, for the same Apostle says: 'When this mortal thing hath put on immortality, then shall come to pass the saying that is written: Death is swallowed up in victory.' Hence the revered Mother of God, from all eternity joined in a hidden way with Jesus Christ in one and the same decree of predestination, immaculate in her conception, a most perfect virgin in her divine motherhood, the noble associate of the divine Redeemer who has won a complete triumph over sin and its consequences, finally obtained, as the supreme culmination of her privileges, that she should be preserved free from the corruption of the tomb and that, like her own Son, having overcome death, she might be taken up body and soul to the glory of heaven where, as Queen, she sits in splendor at the right hand of her Son, the immortal King of the Ages" (Pius XII, *Apostolic Constitution Munificentissimus Deus*).

St. Francis de Sales, Doctor of the Church, wrote: "'You are dust, and to dust you shall return.' This was said to the first Adam and to the first Eve (cf. Gen. 3:19). The second Adam and the second Eve were free from that sentence. The Mother of God died of love, and the love of Her Son raised her up again. This Ark was made of incorruptible acacia wood (cf. Exod. 25:10), just like the ancient Ark. If the ancient Ark was received so solemnly, what must we think of the new Ark? Upon entering heaven, the Virgin, into her Son's royal court, brought with her so much gold of charity, so many perfumes of devotion and virtue, such a quantity of precious stones of patience and sufferings that she had carried in His Name, that we can truly say never has such a treasure been brought into heaven" (St. Francis de Sales, *Sermons on Our Lady: The Assumption of the Blessed Virgin Mary*).

Faced with the pervasive materialism of modern times, Mary's bodily Assumption sheds light on the spiritual and supernatural destiny of mankind: "While the illusory teachings of materialism and the corruption of morals that follows from these teachings threaten to extinguish the light of virtue and to ruin the lives of men by exciting discord among them, in this magnificent way all may see clearly to what a lofty goal our bodies and souls are destined. Finally it is our hope that belief in Mary's bodily Assumption into heaven will make our belief in our own resurrection stronger and render it more effective" (Pope Pius XII, *Apostolic Constitution Munificentissimus Deus*).

Lord, by the mystery of Mary's Assumption into Heaven, grant us holy popes! Grant us many holy popes! Amen.

THE CORONATION

The Coronation of Our Lady as Queen of Heaven and Earth

"From early times Christians have believed, and not without reason, that she of whom was born the Son of the Most High received privileges of grace above all other beings created by God. He 'will reign in the house of Jacob forever,' 'the Prince of Peace,' the 'King of Kings and Lord of Lords.' And when Christians reflected upon the intimate connection that obtains between a mother and a son, they readily acknowledged the supreme royal dignity of the Mother of God" (Pius XII, Encyclical *Ad caeli reginam*).

From the truth that Our Lady is Queen of Heaven and Earth follows her extraordinary power as Mediatrix and intercessor: "For from her union with Christ she attains a radiant eminence transcending that of any other creature; from her union with Christ she receives the royal right to dispose of the treasures of the Divine Redeemer's Kingdom; from her union with Christ finally is derived the inexhaustible efficacy of her maternal intercession before the Son and His Father." (Pope Pius XII, Encyclical *Ad caeli reginam*).

"Far above all the angels and all the saints so wondrously did God endow her with the abundance of all heavenly gifts poured from the treasury of his divinity that this mother, ever absolutely free of all stain of sin, all fair and perfect, would possess that fullness of holy innocence and sanctity than which, under God, one cannot even imagine anything greater, and which, outside of God, no mind can succeed in comprehending fully" (Pius IX, Bull *Ineffabilis Deus*).

As Queen of Heaven and Earth, seated at the right hand of her Only-Begotten Son, Jesus Christ — and truly our mother — Mary devotes herself to our salvation and keeps watch over the entire human race. With her maternal prayers, she pleads most effectively, obtains what she requests, and cannot be refused.

Mary has an almost immeasurable power in the distribution of graces, and is omnipotent in her supplication (see Leo XIII, Encyclical *Adiutricem populi*).

Expressing how happy and greatly honored we are to have, as our true Mother, the Queen of Angels and of all humanity, would be beyond the power of words to capture. Let us remember that at this very moment there is a living heart in Heaven that beats with the most tender maternal love for each of us, no matter how weak and miserable we may be. Hence, we have the duty to imitate our Mother and Queen. St. Thérèse of the Child Jesus used to say: "The Blessed Virgin is Queen of Heaven and Earth, but she is more Mother than Queen." She also wrote: "O Mary, if I were Queen of Heaven and you were Thérèse, I would want to be Thérèse so that you could be the Queen of Heaven!" (*Carnet Jaune*, 21.8.3).

May we thus greet our Mother and Queen with the sublime words of that same saint:

"While I await heaven, oh, my dear Mother, I want to live with you, follow you every day" (*Poésies de Thérèse*, 54).

Lord, by the mystery of the Coronation of Mary as Queen of Heaven and Earth, grant us holy popes! Grant us many holy popes! Amen.

About the Author

Bishop Athanasius Schneider is one of the foremost defenders of Catholic orthodoxy today. He is a prolific author and serves as auxiliary bishop of the Archdiocese of St. Mary in Astana, Kazakhstan, chairman of the Liturgical Commission, and secretary-general of the Conference of Catholic Bishops of Kazakhstan. He is the author of many books, including *The Springtime That Never Came*, *The Catholic Mass*, and the most current and engaging catechism of our time, *Credo: Compendium of the Catholic Faith*.

Sophia Institute

Sophia Institute is a nonprofit institution that seeks to nurture the spiritual, moral, and cultural life of souls and to spread the gospel of Christ in conformity with the authentic teachings of the Roman Catholic Church.

Sophia Institute Press fulfills this mission by offering translations, reprints, and new publications that afford readers a rich source of the enduring wisdom of mankind.

Sophia Institute also operates the popular online resource CatholicExchange.com. *Catholic Exchange* provides world news from a Catholic perspective as well as daily devotionals and articles that will help readers to grow in holiness and live a life consistent with the teachings of the Church.

In 2013, Sophia Institute launched Sophia Institute for Teachers to renew and rebuild Catholic culture through service to Catholic education. With the goal of nurturing the spiritual, moral, and cultural life of souls, and an abiding respect for the role and work of teachers, we strive to provide materials and programs that are at once enlightening to the mind and ennobling to the heart; faithful and complete, as well as useful and practical.

Sophia Institute gratefully recognizes the Solidarity Association for preserving and encouraging the growth of our apostolate over the course of many years. Without their generous and timely support, this book would not be in your hands.

www.SophiaInstitute.com
www.CatholicExchange.com
www.SophiaTeachers.org

Sophia Institute Press is a registered
trademark of Sophia Institute.
Sophia Institute is a tax-exempt
institution as defined by the
Internal Revenue Code, Section 501(c)(3).
Tax ID 22-2548708.